Praise for
Summer of the Oystercatchers

Bryana Joy's *Summer of the Oystercatchers* introduces us to a voice worth befriending, a speaker who we might want to talk with about God over cups of tea. Her diverse subjects (the poems touch on everything from puffins to drone strikes) are held together by a consistently tender gaze. Most impressively, *Summer of the Oystercatchers* manages the tricky feat of being earnest without slipping into territory that is saccharine or shallow. These poems seamlessly pivot between explorations of nostalgia, affection, and love and moments of anger, questioning, and insistence (particularly, insistence on a healthy vision of God and an awareness of the horrors of the world). Even when these poems buzz with frustration or dread, Bryana's tenderness never feels far behind. "I want all the people I've ever friended / to come to my house with their stories, / their offspring, their pictures of God," Bryana writes. If you're anything like me, you'll finish this book feeling like you've also been ushered into the experience of that warm and personal gathering.

–Megan McDermott
author of *Jesus Merch: A Catalog in Poems*,
Woman as Communion, and *Prayer Book for Contemporary Dating*

Summer of the Oystercatchers is a beautiful collection of poetry, its arresting imagery and word play swirling us through the poet's life, childhood to present young adulthood, a book-length dream quest for God's world and its bounty, a blessed, peaceable kingdom, family and friends "circumferenced" around a table—no corners, room enough for all, room for two—a woman and a man, wife and husband—in love for life.

Yes, also a study in Time, how it passes, changing, leaving the poet behind, longing for what, for whom, she dares to believe will surprise her with that knock on her closed door, and she—

Of course it's a spiritual quest to reclaim a land held in the poet's heart, a land "grown tiny and / tender and haunted." She acknowledges "the danger of loving fragile things," asking "why everything / loveable is perishable." She would take the world in her arms—"every warm and frightened / animal body," reclaiming the lost, "coming as fast as I can." *Please live.*

And she refuses to accept any answer to the question of why there is violence in the world, a world of "insatiable wolves," warheads from Hellfire missiles aiming for whole families, their children. The violence of men against women. The tears of the world's sisters. The "good earth" carrying "every child's bone," babies "passed wailing over / a barbed wire fence / in a home pocked by bombs." *Lord have mercy*, the poet cries. "We're not / meant to seal our ears to all this bleating." Yes, she says, *"we can do better,"* her answer to violence, echoing Viktor Frankl's insistence that we are being questioned "daily and hourly" by life, with our answer to what life expects from us being "in right action and in right conduct" (from Frankl's *Man's Search for Meaning*), the poet's answer also affirming what God wants—*not* blood, *not* "the camps the / nighttime raids the cattle prods"; what the poet expects from God is *mercy*; "how lonely it is possible to be," the "lord Jesus at [her] elbow" amening, "isn't that the truth," and God listening when she says, "look at the black trees sprouting / white lace look at the stars / in their fields." And God will look.

How fitting that *Summer of the Oystercatchers* ends with the poet's reacquaintance with God: "Me and God are good buddies actually," big fans of "Planet Earth," its summer weather evenings, the "heathered hills" of rabbits, "piping plovers," and most importantly all those silenced "sisters from history" now invited to sit down with "Me and God" and speak their "unraveled minds." And the sun is not dying. The "shining world / is full of light," and "the cows, / too, go on flicking their tails with / astonishing spunk under the orange sky." And, guess what, the Time Line can snap, preserving the "spunky . . . union of unlike things," woman and man, wife and husband owning each other "with the tenderest care." Now when her husband's step "sounds in the hall at last / each sad thing will unhappen / all at once," and she will lean into him "like a pearl in the / wet heart of an oyster," this couple flourishing "foolish / and happy and found."

–Dr. Robert A. Fink
author of *Strange You Never Knew*, *Beyond Where the West Begins*,
The Tongues of Men and of Angels, *The Ghostly Hitchhiker*, and *Azimuth Points*

Summer of the Oystercatchers

poems

Bryana Joy Beaird

Summer of the Oystercatchers

poems

©2025 by Bryana Joy Beaird

Fernwood Press
Newberg, Oregon
www.fernwoodpress.com

All rights reserved. No part may be reproduced for any commercial purpose by any method without permission in writing from the copyright holder.

Printed in the United States of America

Cover and page design: Mareesa Fawver Moss
Cover image: Pete Godfrey via Unsplash

ISBN 978-1-59498-188-3

for Alex, my harbor

Contents

Praise for *Summer of the Oystercatchers* 1
I. Summer of the Oystercatchers 13
    On the Cusp of the Pandemic 14
    Three Things You Need to Get Through a Plague 15
    The Table 16
    Free Pears 18
    Campus East 20
    Summer of the Oystercatchers 21
    End Time 22
    King's Cross Station 24
    10 Things I Learned in the '10s 25

II. The Mandalina Tree 29
    Kukla Kebap 30
    The Club of Imaginary Friends 32
    Write a Poem About Coffee 34
    At Last I Have It Out with France 36
    Wherever You Go Someone Has Been There Already 38
    Annie 40
    An Ode to Everything 42

Vibrant Photos That Show What
   the Middle East Is Really Like 44
Alterations 46
Aşure (*Noah's Pudding*) 49
Belen Köy 50
The Mandalina Tree 53

III. Tiny Poems for Afghanistan 55
Kabul Airport 56
to the people saying *but i was
   only a child when we invaded Afghanistan* 57
your passport country 58
Long Live the Protestors in Dasht-e Barchī 59
Two Blessings for the Citizens of an Empire 60
One Kabul University Student Said 61
when I see another woman in
   Afghanistan has killed herself 62
On the 20th Anniversary of 9/11 a
   Lot of People Are Saying Never Forget 63
When Anyone Speaks Up for the
   Bombs I Want to Shout: 64

IV. The Lizard King 65
Arrival 66
Hotel Window 67
On Not Losing You After All 68
Collage of Airports 69
Metamorphosis 70
Social Exchange Theory 71
Third Culture 72
The Lizard King 74
Flourish: A Spencerian Definition 76
Angry Dads 79
Flipper 81

Wilfredo Speaks	82
Unnecessary Promise	84

VI. Astronauts in Denmark 85

Astronauts in Denmark	86
Pulling Teeth	87
Nightingale	88
Pet Hates	89
Reindeer Cyclones	91
Puffins	92
Beach Days in Off Season	94
The Multi-Faceted Gem of Forgiveness Catches the Light	95
Lovesong with the Patriarchy Receding in the Distance	96
So long to the ladycage	97

VII. What God Wants 99

Fourteen Reasons Not to Jump	100
Man's Search for Meaning	101
Roofless	102
Jackals	103
Sleet	105
Sure There's a God	106
What God Wants	107
Me and God are good buddies actually,	108
Look	109

VIII. And Winks 111

manifesto on the lifting of a lockdown	112
Acknowledgments	113
Notes	115
Title Index	117
First Line Index	121

I. Summer of the Oystercatchers

On the Cusp of the Pandemic

in the grocery store tonight
the persnickety cashier
smiled at me as though I were
a so-loved friend she knew
she would not see again

the sun was going down
the sky was pink and full of wind
O world I want to take you
in my arms: the trees the colors
the seas full of pufferfish

every warm and frightened
animal body that relies on the
rhythm two lungs make to go on
being the thing that it is

Three Things You Need
to Get Through a Plague

You need three things to get through a plague, and
toilet paper is none of them. Experts are saying this too.

You need rituals: one incomparable cantata in your ears
at all times; raspberry, because it means merry only to you;

blue, if that's your thing. You should go through every day
wearing sky and wave from that ocean you especially love.

Yes, I do know the heart of us each is a small black coal
needing the touch of another's red finger to glow on

but I want you to wake up in the morning—tomorrow,
next week, or when I've been gone from you ten years—

sure of a shining something that you and no other can do,
dear in doing a something that needs you to do it.

You need a wide place in blossom behind your eyes,
a country deeper than coast. It must be a spot you'd be

happy to home in for one infinity if you have to—two
at the most. There should be nightingales there and

roses and all the things needful for life. You must not
leave it, no matter how many stands of snowdrops

bubble and wilt on the hill, the thin years of silence
running into each other. I am coming as fast as I can.

The Table

There is a loneliness in loose ends. All my friends
have gone away with their secret sadnesses, their
hollow spots. We are carrying the things we didn't say.
I didn't say *I too am frightened and asking questions.*
I could have sat beside you in our small apartment,
put out my hands, let in honesty like the stranger
that's an angel (but no one knows it). There was an
awful query hanging in the air. I could have posed it.
God, I have since discovered, would not have minded
a bit. Boys who became my brothers—you all know
who you are—you have every one of you saved my
life like a plumb line, like a star. It was never a thing
I knew how to say. God, how I miss your faces! Harrison
with his T-Rex tees and Offner with his braces; Aaron
with all the questions; Herbst with the holy writ; Chase,
did you know you were just what I needed right when
I needed it? Once, on the threshold of winter, the sky
opened one white eye, winked in the general direction
of God, spilled snow. Remember how we left our books
on the library's third floor, everyone suddenly reckless
and nobody afraid? In the Caf we made it our policy
to sit only at round tables. This was so we could say
there's always room—pull up a chair! But after five
hundred lunches and all of our lingering after, I still
feel I hardly knew you. And now I can't, cause you're
not there. Last year I went back to the village by the
sea. How thin he'd grown, my pudgy, priceless friend!
Time and cigarettes were eating him alive; a churning
blade had chewed on both his feet. Three minutes
passed. We talked about small things. And parted,
and the dark without a sound filled up the space.

I am carrying the voices of my friends: the ways they've
sounded on the phone, the ways their breath has
filled my ears, the ways their tongues have tripped to
tell me they're alone. If, as the soul of everyone seems
in its soul to insist, there is something behind the
curtain after all, my bet is on a table, round as a rainbow
bubble, flat as a ripping frisbee skipping a wall. When
we pull our chairs up to it, we will find we are next
to each other, everyone next to everyone, life in its
prime. The clocks will stop. At last there will be time.

Free Pears

On a fence
in a sagging alley
a sign shouts
FREE PEARS!

There is some
thing too tender
for words in the way
a crowd parts

for a screaming
ambulance. I wish
I could bottle up
that sweep of

silent goodwill.
I'd wear it as a
charm, administer
it like medicine.

As a child, I
faithfully watered
and fed a tiny
white bunny

with a cotton
heart, carried it
with me always
in an Ottoman

coin purse. It
still remembers
secrets even I
have forgotten.

In the rain
a man is carrying
a bonsai tree
next to his chest.

My mother
doesn't have to
keep animals
anymore, but she

persists: a pair of
goats, two cats,
ten chickens and a
honeybee hive.

At times
it's almost like
we were made
to whisper

please live.

Campus East

In that springtime of long walks, I was always saying *Look*
pulling at you to pause for a predictable ecstasy like
Oh the hyacinths are out! or *THIS will be our picnic place. The
 daffodils.*

When the world becomes so small, everything small
takes on stature. The hillock atop the rise took on a city of
rabbits. Puddles took on tadpoles. Black slugs took on names.

You said if by some accident I turned into only a head with
nothing attached, all would be well still. The swallows came
back from Africa and each eave turned peppy with their nesting.

So few things go as planned. In the end, we left without taking
even one picnic in the corridor of yellow trumpets, never
even once sipped our tea ringed by that fringe and fragrance.

But I regret nothing. You said you would slip the little
oval of me into a mesh bag every morning and bring it along.
You said no leg, no limb could come between us.

Summer of the Oystercatchers

Every day that summer
we circled the big lake in our shoes
while the sun was going down slowly
and the starlings were massing.

>   In my hand, your hand was a home fire
>   I could carry with me
>
>   and the geese
>   snipping the grass next to their young.
>
>   From the tops of the buildings, two oystercatchers
>   nightly called for one another
>   in their language of wide seas.
>   O

why is it
anything that can love you back has skin full of veins
and a beating heart that must stop
beating?

When I found one of them on the shore,
its gorgeous lips parted and its
wings stiff with mud,
I did not tell you
though a stone settled into my throat.

I am asking why everything
loveable is perishable. I am
asking about the oystercatchers with their
beautiful mouths. I am
not going to accept any answer.

End Time

In my dream last night someone
        had punched the red button at last.
I don't know who it was that did it
        in the end. Was it us? Was it them?

I only know a handful of people on this
        planet, most of them kind.
I only know *pigeon* and *dove* are two words
        for the same winged creature.

At the window in our high-rise apartment
        we saw it coming.
(What would you do if you had only
        thirty seconds to live? This is a question

I have never been asked, never spent
        any time thinking of.)
All around us the buildings were going down
        with the people still in them.

They had not yet said what they needed to
        say or done what they promised.
The children would never again be told *stop*
        slipping shells of sliced bread

to the birds in the park. Bye-bye birds.
        Bye-bye bread. I always enjoyed
the warm mushroom smell you made
        and the oven door banging. I also liked

butter, black tea, and Vivaldi, and how
    do you say your *I love yous*
when the world has run out of agains?
    On the carpet where we clung to each other

with no time left, I looked at your hands and
    they were two full cups.
Your eyes were full of wings. There was
    enough——

King's Cross Station

all night we were crossing the ocean
none of us could see
through the dark egg windows
far below us the baleen were
rolling in the deep we
were tired but could not sleep

still the morning arrived at her appointed hour
the trains were on their tracks
we held in our hands warm
bread huge luggage
above us a board was blinking orange
numbers not meaning anything
we could understand

in that country
I was the only one you knew
you were the only one I knew
no one noticed us
sitting for hours or was it days
under the domed skylights with the pigeons
at our feet hearing the journeys
ending and beginning
with soft clicking sounds
in a pink place

if anything takes you
away from me and you do not know
where to go

go there

10 Things I Learned in the '10s

1.

God is speaking to us but
in a foreign language.

2.

In all the world there is no oak tree
like the one in your village. You called it
by a name and watched summer
and thunder come through its leaves.
When you leave, it is standing there still,
a tree worth more than other trees.
Things are not equal, but they can be.

3.

Never hush the small mouth in your heart
when it cries out that what is right must be better.
Kiss that small mouth. It is your one true love.

4.

To say with shining eyes "because of you" to a man
need be no kind of idolatry.
A man's violence may do violence to the Deity in your eyes.
Why shouldn't another man by speaking softly heal it?

5.

A body that used to belong to a name
is a hole in the universe through which stars leak
even if he was only a large, blond dog
who smelled like an old puddle

and ravaged each new plot of petunias
as fast as they went into the ground.
For days you will think about his stone on the hill
with a mad loneliness nothing can touch.
This is our best cause for hope.

6.

Whatever you may have heard,
things are not getting worse and worse,
only different and different.
Each difference must be assessed
on its own merits. For example:
babies couched in a wasteland
of blue lights. For example:
some women bubble their ballots
edge to edge, firm as a handshake,
full as a floodlight; their grandmothers
believed this day would come.

7.

In spite of everything, don't lose your faith
in a table circumferenced with friends.

8.

It is easy to forgive almost anyone you knew
when they were a child and the two of you
played tag until twilight in a knot of belonging
and poured in fat inner tubes down the sugared hill
and there was never enough time, never.

9.

The way things look matters less and less
when it becomes apparent that you will die.
Today, tomorrow, or in seventy years, but certainly
before you can prepare it for houseguests,
you must hand over the keys to your soul.
In the end, not one of our secrets will be kept.

10.

When your eyes have softened to whatever they see,
you will begin to understand what She is saying.

II. The Mandalina Tree

Kukla Kebap

there is a wounded thing inside me going on about
something but I do not know what it is
going on about

in a long room full of chairs
I wanted my mother to see the marionettes
when I was five and small enough
to be lifted to my father's shoulders

is it going on about the puppets going
up and down on their strings that my mother
never saw even though I looked for her
in all those smoky people and found her
too late

how cold the street was
the taxis coming and going

when my sister turned five
I begged my mother not to get
her a brown baby tortoise that would
eat lettuce and make her too happy to speak

I was seven but I knew already
the danger of loving fragile things

the tortoise of course died in only a week
we had a funeral in a plot of weeds
the high-rise apartments all around us
we wrote epithets on a large gray rock
how much we had to say to this
small shelled animal who was in our house
only a week and almost never
showed its face

we laid its little body in the red dirt
a brittle mustard bush
spilled pods of black seeds

how fast you went away before I was ready
you were saying something but I do not know
what it was

The Club of Imaginary Friends

When we were children we knew very few people
who spoke our language.

When guests came over I sat up as late as they would let me,
straining to make sense of politics and theology, always stuck
on terms like *cinsel* and *piç*—mystery words I knew
I wasn't allowed to understand.

For years my sister
     who was not yet two when her world switched
     tongues
tuned out everything but English.
     We had each other

and thirty-five square feet of smooth concrete
just in view of the apartment window   from which
Mom could see us and from which   all distances were measured.

We had two small bikes   with red and blue tires   that became
noble steeds with names and temperaments of their own.   And

     we had all the people we'd ever met
     to keep us company.

     Oh cousins who we visited once every two-and-a-
half years and were slightly scared of even though
we all wanted to like each other—
     Oh friends of the children of our parents' friends
who we saw only once at a birthday party and
didn't have the courage to speak to—

     we had you.

If we met you one time in America
and you made even an indifferent impression on us,
you can be sure you were a member of our
Club of Imaginary Friends.
You accompanied us on a hundred hijinks,
pounded bareback over prairies peppered
with covered wagons, purple bonnets, buffalo.
You fought crime on three or four continents,
solved cases that would have baffled
Encyclopedia Brown, boy detective.
You have lived a whole life you don't even
    know about.

Write a Poem About Coffee

Coffee first came onto my scene when I was six,
courtesy of a pair of Australian expats packing
their bags. My parents got a modest countertop
machine. I got Peter Slater's 1999 pocket planner,

Australian Birds; a treasury of song and feathers;
a hardback sliver of a book I would carry with me
from one continent to the next, always about to become
an ornithologist, an Audubon, a better bird-watcher.

How quickly medium-roast became integral to
mornings! That Christmas, we had to wait for more
than the mellowing glow of sunrise to fill our windows.
On the floor in the family room we sat under the

winking tree and waited for steam and drip to end
in gurgle and snort and velvet aroma. And on every
January first of childhood, I would weigh the same
question: *Could this be the year to use Australian Birds?*

Thumbing its glossy pages, I didn't mind that 1999 was
past recall, that it would be 11 years before another
April 12 Easter. But something is unsettling about a
flag-planting. It's brash, too sure of the moment.

Today I pay the rent with paintbrushes. Sometimes
I accidentally rinse them in the tall latte next to my
water cup. I reassure myself that watercolors aren't
toxic. I am occasionally embarrassed by how little

I have learned about Australia. On my last birthday
we waited for our drinks under a wall map delineating
the world's coffee-growing regions, wondered aloud
about the omission of Australia's southern side.

Are there cold patches in the sunburnt country? What
makes the galahs go pink? Where are the shelducks
winging to, so chestnut and so green? Their beaks
are turned into the squall. They are breasting a

deepening gray, but they do not seem worried. If I
was like them, I could say goodbye to you every day
without this black pebble in my throat. Can you guess
why the stormy petrel carries Saint Peter's name?

As a child I confess I smuggled Peter Slater over the
ocean more than once, fitting him into my suitcase
among folded layers of denim and cotton tees.
Once you find joy, you want it always beside you.

At Last I Have It Out with France

I do not want to have anything against you, France,
you field of lavender against a sky of peaches.
Give my love to Enjolras, the one who got away.
Also Debussy has always been there for me,
in his outstretched hands a magic box
lined with sage velveteen and full of fairies.
      But we must talk
      about your effect
      on the relatives.

I don't know why all the
mean cousins who came
to visit our friends in the summers
came from France.
It is a puzzle that has been gnawing
at the back of my mind
like a termite munching on a
fine house in the suburbs,
chewing up the floorboards, the
furniture, leaving behind only
golden ovals of cellulose as
smooth as sesame seeds.

In my defense, we all have memories
sticking to us, the buttons of barnacles
on the slimy hull of an ocean liner. And I
have a rhinoceros beetle as big as an egg
stuck to my glasses, a flurry of black legs
flung by a French cousin.

In the Paris airport a woman
who could have smiled at me didn't
and I have held it against her ever since.
Also, the walls were unfinished,
bare as an empty mailbox shuttered
by a spiderweb.
I was eight and expected
kindness everywhere.

*Rhinoceros beetles have become
popular pets in parts of Asia
due to being relatively clean,
easy to maintain, and safe
to handle.*

But in the night
I wake up sometimes with one eye
blocked by a black thorax,
in my chest a soundless
quivering scream.

I have always felt that you were partly to blame.
Please talk me out of it.

> I am
> an educated woman
> [and I do not want to have prejudices]

Wherever You Go Someone
Has Been There Already
for Paul Shackelford

All these years the clouds have been falling
into the Mulberry River like white milk thinned
and choppy and now
we have come.

We are still too young to make a fuss about things
like the blue spread of blood under the skin
or the stilted tracks of scrapes or slime
slick on stones.

We come without instruments because after all
this young person needs nothing but himself:
his firm, supple flesh, and the lodestar in his breast.
We are not afraid

of frail, quiet people or the hostile vines,
the scratched faces of cliffs, the tight trees.
We let the cold close around our chests, and we break
with the monstrosity of maps.

We will go to a place where no one has been before.
From a rock no other bared leathery feet
have hugged, we shall look down with scorn
on ordinary things,

on the little pink figures sunning with their
fingers parted to wave and their lips wide,
on the cloudy river curling like a tame snake
through the humps of the hills.

We went up with our hearts like songbirds.
On the far side of sanity and fences we might have found
anything: a dragon with icicle teeth or even
the edge of the world.

The unknown is a range of rejoicing.
We slowed when our toes touched a ribbon of asphalt
and a high, familiar monster came at us
on eighteen wheels, trumpeting.

Annie

They brought her home in hazelnut season,
the sweet sad end of summer, and I knew
we weren't going to be friends.

In the orchards the raspy branches
were browning with clustered nuts. Annie
couldn't make pancakes,

her pancakes were fat and stuck
to the skillet and grew black spots. Mom
spoke to her warmly and laughed

like it didn't matter. Between the bookshelves
they drank coffee and talked about things
I wasn't old enough to hear.

September came on like a scent on the air,
the sky growing heavy, a promise of rain.
On the hillsides, hazelnuts

in their pale green husks. The sun. Annie
wanted to come too even though
she didn't know how to do anything,

didn't know how to fill a feed sack with
spiny leaf casings or bear sunburn or sit
in a shaded circle of heat and hijabs

eating salty goat cheese and tahini helva in
tiny slivers, cherishing the sugar on her
tongue. When she asked if we could

leave soon, I smiled on her benevolently
like an indulgent parent. All night the neighbors
husked hazelnuts on the concrete

outside their house, downing red tea
from fluted glasses. When the clouds broke,
bringing the cold, blue tarps came out

like umbrellas. My dreams were full
of their laughter. Of rain. Annie
took a plane out of Istanbul

back to where she belonged. When I think
of her now, I remember how she wrote
letters to her boyfriend every night

in big loopy print with hearts. The next year,
a great orange husking machine
with a hose like an elephant's trunk

rolled through the village and spit out
smooth nuts, a fountain of marbles,
a job one woman can now do in an hour.

An Ode to Everything

If you could go back, you would write
an ode to everything.

An ode to the dishwasher with the prongs
snapping off, dying of a rust disease—

it is like every other dishwasher: it is a
white cube in the kitchen.

An ode to the kitchen, pink and tiled and
smelling like hot vinegar, like cinnamon,

like mint, like unwashed vegetables with
earth clinging to them, like the black earth.

An ode to the black earth, to the purple thyme,
to the time that came to visit us and left

while we were not looking. An ode to the
children that were everywhere, although

the significance was sometimes lost on you.
An ode to the children that have been lost.

An ode to scaling wooded heights in our sweat.
An ode to sweat. An ode to soap. An ode to love.

No matter that no one will listen,
that everyone will listen, no matter

that they will stare, they who have never
been long enough away to grow new eyes.

You would stand up on the frail, sticky table
and feel an ode coming on: Ode to a Table.

But it is not a table. It is the table, scarred
by acrylic paints, watered orchids, drops

of candlelight. An ode to the table steeped in
white cakes, in sunny guitar.

You say, God, we were so happy.
God, you say, because everything else is changed.

Vibrant Photos That Show What the Middle East Is Really Like
(title of January 18, 2019 VICE article highlighting photographer Ali Al-Shehabi)

In every way he can, he is saying his country is beautiful too.
The curls of carnation against the wall are witness,
the gold-headed *gahwa* cups peering over each other
parse this riot of tenderness:

> open Quran resting in the crook of the *rehal*,
> the black hair on the model's head and legs and arms,
> gray boxers over which his belly only just begins to spill,
> that scent of coffee, that white Saturday on the walls.

And I don't for a minute doubt him.
I also hold a land in my heart

>   as sweet as the last sip of amber *çay*
> in a tulip glass with the sugar cube still crumbling
>   as joyous as a cross-legged meal on the carpet,
> everyone eating from the same dish
>   as hearty as a haul of hazelnuts
> being husked through the night in a circle of song
>   as golden as hot *lokma*
> in a borrowed bowl
>   as generous as yellow plums appearing
> like bulbs of summer light
>   as sparse as a little boy with no pants
> peering over a wall of smashed oil cans
>   as impaired as the *amca*'s one milky eye
> when he said *keep a stick on her back and a child in her belly*.

When I was eleven, I stepped into a room
full of a table covered with
a thousand parted lips and pairs of glowing legs,
piles of arched backs, little waists, bubble breasts;
on all the walls, chairs
occupied by men
filling ashtrays, flipping pages.
I went into the street, walked   a long time
though I had nowhere to go.

Alterations

I.

The day suddenly comes,
the day feared and hoped for.

At the sink the seamstress
dries her dark hands.

One by one I slip my legs
into the white fountain.

Charmeuse clings to them
like a refugee

clings to a motherland. The
cold pins arch my back.

II.

When you get married, they said
in the village by the sea

*we'll dance all night and
paint your skin with henna.*

On the hillside under my
window, summer nights

were full of songs. They said
this is your home now.

III.

The seamstress says *stand a
little straighter*, her mouth

full of pins, her accent thick
with African French. I want

her to talk about the Congo, but
how can anyone ask for that?

IV.

I remember how the bride would sit
under the red scarf

and cry softly—an old custom,
a way to say goodbye.

Sometimes a modern bride
needed a sly onion slice

slipped under the veil.
But some didn't. I remember

being twelve saying I didn't want
to get married if I had to cry.

V.

*What do you miss the most
about the Congo?* I ask.

The seamstress takes my buttons
out of their little loops.

Well, she says. She hesitates.
She has a good job here she says

she is so thankful, and I know
she is remembering something

she will not be able to tell me.

Aşure (*Noah's Pudding*)

When he walked off the ark after
deluge, slosh, and antsy bird-watching,
there wasn't much left in the way of
edibles. This, at least, is the story the
Turkish people tell, ladle in hand.
There's no recipe for *aşure*. You can
add rice and rosewater and garnets
of pomegranate. You can let coconut
drift over the filberts like snow.

I want all the people I've ever friended
to come to my house with their stories,
their offspring, their pictures of God.
One Polaroid shows a huge toe poised
over a sugar ant. Another is nothing
but fog on a road, an endless white sky.
A man plays a violin, and every note
sprouts wings. A child with red eyes
watches a small candle blink.

There's no recipe for *aşure*, but I
like it with cinnamon, chickpeas,
scant fig, and lucent apricot. I like
the way the raisins get blimpy again
after all that boiling in lemon and
white beans. I like the way you open
your door, and a neighbor you hardly
know kisses both your cheeks, cries
Run, get a bowl! I made this for you.

Belen Köy

After years had sprouted, withered,
and died between us, I took planes, trains,
buses, a shuttle, a car, and came back
over the cloudy ocean, through the
flat city full of coal smoke, rounded the
mountain pass with its rainy hat.

In the home of my childhood, everything
is my darling: the hillocks, the rosehip
bush, the yellow plums. I want to hug the
ground to me; it smells like a thousand
Septembers; it's a cocklebur war; it's the
rain that always comes.

Come in, they tell me, *he will be glad
to see you.* I grow older. I already know
how it will be. I leave my shoes in a
stairwell smoggy with cigarettes and
step in. There are but few promises
we are permitted to keep.

Under the coverlet, both the feet of my
childhood friend are mangled, mauled
by a toothed machine in an accident.
He used to infuriate me with his
made-up rules for football and his fluid
forward rolls on the pocked cement;

and his habit of inattention to his
homework; and his way of saying *later*
without saying when; and his way of
counting unreasonably fast to forty in
Hide & Seek Freeze Tag; and his hints
of becoming a man like other men.

I grow older. I think I am coming to
understand it. All that could be could
never have really been. We find each other
again to find we no longer speak the
same language, and there's much to be
said but no tongue to say it in.

The valley I love has grown tiny and
tender and haunted; it's a ghost town,
a favorite doll with a missing limb. As we
pass back through it, my fingers are
folded over my soul mate's fingers. He is
harbor. All of my ships are docked in him.

I lay my ear on the skin stretched over
his heartbeat. I don't know of a single
secret between us two. But if we had
seventy years to share all the last words we
could think of, there is always something
forgotten; or something new.

There is always something that's running
faster than language. There is always a
wordless thing coming out in front. When
the casket ceiling comes down on a face
you are friends with, the unwordable
thing is a vicious and terrible want.

I am giving up my belief in happy
endings. I give up my belief in endings
of any sort. Surely the soul is the
foremost story—too sweet to fade
to a flyleaf; too atrocious, too dread
to abandon or abort.

The Mandalina Tree

In Adana, the mandalinas are beginning to glow
on their branches like bulbs of warm light.

Twenty Decembers later, and despite a bad year,
a dollar fifty will still get you a ten-pound sack.

I suppose that's why I remember them, cobbled
circle and squirt, shining on the dining table

through every Christmas Day week; piled high,
going fast. That zip and tart is on my tongue still.

I want to make my home in a mandalina tree, to
smell all the time of citrus and the extravagance

of light. To everyone who visits me, I shall hand
a halo of orange, begging *won't you bite into*

how good this world can be? I want to say *war is
over if you want it* and for no one to talk back.

III. Tiny Poems for Afghanistan

Kabul Airport

don't look away
from the scrambling
on the tarmac all those
feet so many feet with
nowhere to go

if you do not have mercy on us lord
i don't blame you but have

mercy on the three small boys
in their red shirts

and every woman

to the people saying
  but i was only a child
  when we invaded Afghanistan

listen   can't you hear
the good earth loving
every child's bone she carries?

when the train came someone
grabbed your hand

we are grown   up now
we made it

your passport country

is nothing to be proud of
did you pick it? no you did not

for all the say you had in the matter
you might as easily have been

a baby passed wailing over
a barbed wire fence
in a home place pocked by bombs

where did those bombs
Come From
i wonder?

Long Live the Protestors in Dasht-e Barchī

i for one am fonder than language
of her in the purple pushing
forward with her mouth
not closed and even her fingers speaking

some people are saying
these are the bravest   women in the world
but i ask you this why

do we have to be so brave
in every place
to be looked at like we too   Belong Here?

Two Blessings for the Citizens of an Empire
after the deadly 08/29/21 U.S. drone strike in Kabul

when you pause for applause
may you grow accustomed
to only the sawing of the crickets

may you see a warhead barreling
from a Hellfire missile making
for a whole family with their ten little dreams
and say good
lord is it i?

One Kabul University Student Said

*They destroyed the only bridge
that could connect me with my future.*

After I read this, I walk all day
through my house full of its shelves,
hearing each book weep.

*How can I react? I believed that I could
study and change my future
or bring the light to my life.*

All day I think about the voices saying,
"Be thankful for what you have."

But all I can be is a loose faucet   no screw will fit.
The tears of my sisters
are an ocean running   out of my mouth.

[The poem title and italicized lines are from the BBC's 21 December 2022 piece: "Taliban ban women from universities amid condemnation."]

when I see another woman in Afghanistan has killed herself

I see faster   I see the rope the rat poison
as fast as I can I see so I can stop   seeing
how old she was   how impossible
it had become to be her
I never think a version of *oh she shouldn't have*
I never think a thing that's not *flowers! send*
them by the busload and with teeth

think about your own city somewhere
there too a holy book has someone
at the end of their rope   please keep
an eye on your holy books   you can't
make God madder than he is right now

On the 20th Anniversary of 9/11 a Lot of People Are Saying Never Forget
(Ankara, Turkey—December 2001)

i never forget the neighbor boy
from the shack city up the street

how he said *have you caught Bin Laden yet?*
and i snatched my gloves from his hands

i never forget the snow falling faster
and faster on that huffy walk home

my pockets were full of mittens
at least three pairs

When Anyone Speaks Up for the Bombs I Want to Shout:

your we is somebody else's they
your us is somebody's them

yes i am talking about
your we with the apple cheeks
and the well-tilled field of hopes
wearing her own colors
into the morning

your darling we who does no wrong for which
there is not an explanation

if you only hear me saying one thing
i hope it's this

IV. The Lizard King

Arrival

for Alex, of course

the day you came
into my
by-myself life

i was still
hoodwinking everyone
most of all me

i was still saying
sword is a good word
though it slit me

i said bitter was
the best taste
but I didn't like it

lonesome made a
last stand
then
you

Hotel Window
after Edward Hopper's painting by the same name

But I was afraid

of how sweet words sour in the press
of the years of the babies of the bills
of our disappointed standards and skin stretching
and the little wrinkles creeping in
of the great void when you go

of the sealed envelope I pressed to the lamp
and found beaming with cursive promises.

The Little Prince has golden hair his smile is
crooked his eyes are green and the wild birds
are flying south. He won't stay.

No one has ever done what they could.
The back alleys in Belfast are filling with rain
like your hair slowly fills up with silver
between the borders of birthdays
when you're not looking.

I could have said yes.

On Not Losing You After All

There are dreams where you feel your lungs filling.
What was I doing? you say when the blue water hits your brain
    What was I doing all my life?

Have the cars come loose on the ski lift over the sharp trees
    a mile over the sharp trees?
Goodbye you say to the good world in which you lived without
    thinking.

I in my sleep kept murmuring broken benedictions to the white
    walls
        whispering *I shall not want*
        but
like a lamb with one ebony hoof in the teeth of a gray wolf.

You open your eyes on the carpet, a heap of sheets over your head.

Collage of Airports

I.

an airport is a city where no one is staying
no one is looking at the streets thinking of
living on them no one is looking up at the windows the
eyes of the houses wondering what is happening behind them
everyone is on their way to somewhere you wonder
where are they going will they get there

II.

when they were spending the last of the sterling
on caprese baguettes with basil he said
I'm so sorry and she said only short words so she would
not weep in front of everyone coming and
going to and from London for their own reasons
words like *okay* like *I'm fine it's okay*

in the air they sit between two sets of sleeve
tattoos and the screens noisy with blood
the engines are filling their ears they talk softly
they wonder if they'll ever arrive

III.

there are lights below me a city of
people in their homes full of lights
I am riding the shadow that is cutting the sky
that is tipping faster and faster *this is the end* I think
as I have many times thought on other days and lived

I hope you know I love you I only said it
ten thousand times

Metamorphosis
after Kafka

what if one morning I woke up and I was
a great black beetle as long as the bed
we've often sat on with the rain at the window
reading softly to each other
the driveway filling with mud

I would be so confused lying with six
fringed legs waving over my head my
huge domed eyes buried in the sheets
eyes full of a thousand dark caves like
the foam in a boombox if I was
a great bug tenderly watching you move
across the room but without words
only my antennae quivering

which wouldn't happen but what if it
    did?

Social Exchange Theory

"Romantic love is seen as resulting when one feels that he or she is getting a high ratio of rewards with little cost. That is, the reward/cost ratio affects how we feel about other people ... Similarly, we fall out of love with those who cost us too much of ourselves."
     —Suzanne R. Smith, *Exploring Family Theories*

When I remember what has passed
through my life
how shadows have encircled it
like hungry wolves
how the world is full of insatiable wolves
I tip my hat to the grave sociologists thinking
their cold thoughts making
perfect sense

but

when I remember how I stood forlorn and selfish
in the kitchen with the sun
splitting the blinds and you walked in
and kissed me and said
you thought you wouldn't go out
with the guys that night after all and I
leaned into you like a pearl in the
wet heart of an oyster
I'm not so sure.

Third Culture

in the end I wonder
what will be left

all my life everyone
has been going away
from me like
the stars hurtling away
from the big bang
they are further apart
every day

in the airports and the
bus stations we have hung on
for the last time making
promises we know we can't keep

some people went without saying
anything at all
there is only a sad feeling in my stomach
when I accidentally remember them
a feeling growing fainter year by year

my grandfather is eighty-four and
wants people to laugh
on the phone he gives me wisdom
for our lives together
he says to tell you
you have good taste in women
a joke for which my nana surely
chides him from the next room
her words bouncing off like raindrops
hitting an umbrella as usual

you set down your classical mythology
on the thick arm of the chair and
cherish my face with your fingers

in woman
you say
I have good taste
in woman

and I am answered at last

The Lizard King

*Would you still love me
        you ask
if I was a lizard king?*
Pretend this shell of my beloved body
holds a kernel of keratin beads
cold, green, and dart-like.
At night it emerges. Imagine
yourself standing when the moon is full
at the window in your sleep shirt, watching
the large reptile of me going by.
Don't leave out anything:
the black snake of my tongue,
the creased sack of my throat.

In the news today: a couple
of centenarians celebrated
eighty-two years of sleeping
in the same bed.
When they were born,
even our grandparents
had not yet been thought of.
Still, when I look in the mirror
sometimes my heart
droops inside me like a
thirsty azalea,
pink and panting.

Remember our chance meeting on the day
when we were most hoping for it?
We saw each other from a long way off.
Our smiles were like synchronized swimmers
blooming underwater into dance.
Yes can be the biggest word.

Flourish: A Spencerian Definition
from the Honeymoon Postcards

1.

It was for a *Daboll's Arithmetick* that he walked so they say
twenty miles barefoot in the backwoods of Ohio, drowsing
in a leaky trailside barn, dining on one sparse raw turnip.
But what we remember are his letters, each line a flock of birds.

2.

a noun: a luxuriant growth, showiness
      in the doing of something

a verb: to be in a vigorous state, to
      embellish with fanciful curves

3.

people also ask:
      Why is cursive not taught anymore?
      Why does cursive exist?

4.

When I awoke on the morning
after our wedding,
I donned a ridiculous hat.
At the port I peered out from under
a newfound ostentation
and six inches of white-weave brim.
It's alright, I said to the
good-looking stranger
who wondered aloud about the
weight of the bags.

My husband will be here soon.
He can't have missed the strut
in my step, the way my chin
perked like a watered hydrangea.

5.

Of course for a time Spencer abhorred himself.
Letters from him came seldom. Alone in his room,
he roved over red rejections with foggy eyes.
I have failed the Lord God he naturally thought
and drained still another bottle because at that point

                                                                            why not?

6.

I think all elevators shafts should be windows,
like the ones running through the bellies of
cruise ships. I want to always remember the
small boys dancing behind the glass,
obstreperous as orangutans in their high trees.
Each hand was a whirl of paper windmill
waving at the decks as they passed.
Each move an exhibition, a way of saying

7.

watch me, watch me!

8.

In Ashtabula County
some of the trees
remember him.

None of a widow's ten
children can afford
paper, a slate, or a pen.

But what is in us
must come out.
If you look closely

at each spot of smooth trunk
you might find a snatch
of his flight plans.

9.

an adjective: foolish
      and happy and found

Historical Note: Platt Rogers Spencer (1800-1864) is known today as the originator of the Spencerian script, one of the most prominent historical forms of cursive penmanship. Spencer was intrigued by beautiful handwriting from childhood and reportedly practiced on leaves, bark, snow, and ice because his family was too poor to afford proper writing materials for him. As a young man, Spencer planned to attend college and study for the ministry. However, his prospects were sabotaged by his increasing dependence on alcohol. He began working as a teacher instead and soon married another teacher. With the help of his wife and a period of rural seclusion, Spencer eventually succeeded in conquering his alcoholism and became a prominent academic and advocate for temperance and abolition. Traditional calligraphers still study and use the Spencerian script, and it is featured in the logos for Coca-Cola and the Ford Motor Company.

Angry Dads
from the Honeymoon Postcards

Here, as everywhere, they seem to pursue us.
The pitch and toss of a day is too much for
them, even a day delectable with sea foam

and shine and the Shots Guy going from table
to table after dinner, flourishing a platter
of sparkle and burn—their favorite things.

On the ship's tender, a human tornado briefs
his whole timid family on the storm he's
preparing. *When I get up, you jump up, you*

follow me, he rumbles. He ain't gon' wait in
no line. Is he a man that he should practice
patience and perspicacity? No. He is blizzard

and typhoon and maelstrom and mad [at
other people for existing and at the Italian
restaurant that can't seat him yet because

all their servers are serving]. Don't paint God
with this brush and expect the gallery to be
full of heart and hush. We've spent enough

time behind the thin doors of shuddering
closets, willing the hinges to hold. No, if I
dared to paint again, I know just the man

I would use for my sable bristles. He dips
himself in so many hues of happiness, peers
into my eyes all the time to ask *isn't this good?*

He is a flying buttress, a buttered pancake,
a thing you can't regret. He is splattered
to the eyebrows with cyan, magenta and joy.

Flipper
from the Honeymoon Postcards

If you do not come up, I will go down after you
even though I have floppy legs and ear drums
as delicate as paper lanterns. I will kick and kick,
I will close my eyes, I will think about frogs,
I will pray *dear God please let me sink*. I know
I will not be able to bring you back through
this much weight and wet. I know once I reach
you in that far green fish country, it will be all
I can do to let my body loosen like a shoelace
and shoot for sky. But I will not come out of this
ocean to your absence. I would much rather
squeeze your wilting hand while our lungs send
their last balloons up, up, bulb-clear and brief.
        O that would not be the worst thing.

Wilfredo Speaks
from the Honeymoon Postcards

Yes I know I have a name that
sounds to you like egg-ribbon
pasta in snow cheese and cream
drip, and when you get home maybe
that's what you'll remember.

But each night I wipe down wine
glasses one fragile stemmed
globe at a time. I set them aside
in a stack of shine, a future of
shatter. I have thoughts.

May I put in a word for mussels
in lemon-butter broth? When steam
probes them, they split their dark
shells and let their tiny hearts
dangle, succulent and soft. Don't

get a heart of lettuce even if
it comes with golden oil and a
punch of black pepper. All the
dressings in the world can't salt
the guarded core of a glacier.

No, if you're set on a salad, can I
point you to a caprese: a speckle of
capers, a twinning of tomatoes and
mozzarella rounds? The union of
unlike things can be flavorful and

fine. Dare I say don't forget this
on the nights when you lay
under separate sections of sheet,
each as raw and pink as a pounded
shaving of carpaccio? Oh let

love be as spunky as spanakopita,
as merry as penne mariscos,
patient as a pot of lobster flushed
with rose (because after all, who
knows?) And whatever comes,

come back. The best is always
saved for last. The foam is turning
at the tail, the muddled middle
times are past. The drowsy waves
are full of moon, the shining world
is full of light. It doesn't have to be
goodbye. It might only be goodnight.

Unnecessary Promise

when we are parted I will leave
each thing the way it is
no matter what the grief counselor tells me
with the best intentions

this is not madness for I know
when I sit down to each dinner I have made for only one
only one is there

yet what sheets I slip under
in any country are ours
and yearn for you
turning over in the dark

each door I locked after you entered
has its ears peeled for your knock
it expects nothing from the future
besides wondrous you

when your step sounds in the hall at last
each sad thing will unhappen
all at once

VI. Astronauts in Denmark

Astronauts in Denmark

*First All-Female Spacewalk Canceled Because NASA
Doesn't Have Two Suits That Fit*
   —*The New York Times*, March 25, 2019, headline

It had to be a bad day for whomever had the job
of announcing that the first all-female spacewalk was
off, citing the shortage of suits in the right size.

They had to know they would be laying a
finger on the softly seeping wound of history
and pushing it in, past the ruptured curtain

of the dermis and right into a red well of troubles.
A call to compassion: it must be hard
to be always hurting people and not knowing

how to stop. You are like Laertes, the kind and
cocksure brother. You leave home the way a lion
heads to a water hole, his mane filled with light,

his every step even. Even the sun adores
you, loads your coat with gold each morning.
It cannot be your fault, surely, that the world

wants you to taste everything she has got.
When you come home, the house is dark,
the wind is up, the water high. And you know

already, without knowing how, that you have
lost your sister, your oldest and best friend.
Even the stars hear it, your long howl of keening.

Pulling Teeth

Victorian women were warned to expect a tooth loss
for each baby they wrung out of that tired pink canal.
Gain a child, lose a tooth! medical wisdom and matrons said,
implying that, while grim, it was more than a fair trade.

As a medical profession, dentistry was a late bloomer, a
somewhat frivolous field. Barbers, after all, were already
doing a fine job plucking by lamplight the bared gums
of wailing patients who were bolted to their chairs.

My Yorkshire friend tells me it was once considered a
handsome thing for a father to fund the full removal of
his marriageable daughter's teeth. And I mean, who
doesn't want the most hassle-free bride they can find?

After the Battle of Waterloo, the price of false teeth
plummeted. I often think about those acres of rigid blue
bodies, each plundered gum ragged, and how in every
age there have been people saying *suck it up, buttercup.*

On Monday a surgeon with an unusually high number of
*A*s in his name extracted impacted molars from my little
sister's mouth. When she came to, she cried and dribbled
blood full of bubbles but felt ordinary in only an hour.

On Tuesday news reached us that Dr. Alaaaldin Radwan
had hydroplaned on the wet highway and hit a tree, a
thing that happens. I am frightened every day but have
determined to be one of the people saying *we can do better.*

Nightingale

At any given time it's a tall order to find God,
but in the spring of 1790, I know where I'd look first.
Back at Monticello, Sally is going on seventeen.
She strokes her taut belly in a room with no windows,
and it's in that place I imagine the Holy Spirit is perched,
not dove this time but nightingale.

The nightingale is not what you expect.
Unlike the operas it inspires, it's no eye-catcher.
You won't notice it sitting brown in the coppice,
tucked up the way a homely secret is stowed in a great house.

Soon someone will be hollering *Push harder, child! Push!*
way down in Egypt land. Sally knows what it's like
to own nothing that can be touched,
not even her own fledgling body.

Not until you silence your large and well-lit home
will you hear it: up and down the swampy dark,
a thousand golden throats.

Pet Hates

> *"Every time you press a button on the device or on the remote, the fan BEEPS VERY LOUDLY, just a pet hate of mine."*
> —Amazon Customer Review

Just a pet hate, of which I have many. They do no harm and give me much comfort in this desolate world. Here comes one now, plucky and panting, fresh from hounding the rabbits in the hedge. His nose is a wet button and he wants to be fondled. This one is the way I feel about houses with small windows, country without trees, and all those people who wouldn't try a real book if you wrapped it in bacon and deep-fried it. See how I cosset him under his collar and daily toss him the bones of my discontent? At night, he sleeps next to my socks like a capped bottle of bubbles—
    as buoyant and as hungry for heights.

And there are others. A fingernail jaw unfolds to plead for a pinch of ink-eyed krill. She's my loathing for drive-thrus and phone calls to the bank. If you tap the glass, you can watch her wane into her keratin husk, the red banners over her earspots retreating like routed cavaliers. Behind a lattice of white bars, my contempt for a particular orange man is making ardent music, an aria with room for other enmities. Listen, and you'll hear how I feel about the strange immunity we give the rapists on our own team, political or ball. Abhorrence of priests and pop-stars
    is in that incisive snap of seeds.

On the whole, my pets are a good set, and cause very little trouble, aside from the small nuisances their continuous neediness occasions: rigid feeding schedules, cleaning of cages and suchlike. Sometimes the fish eat each other. But that's normal. I'll tell you a strange thing. There's a big one around here somewhere, but

I haven't seen it in months. Used to be in that tank against the wall and then one day it wasn't. Sometimes when the house is still, the dishes done, and all the doors bolted, I swear I sense a slow bulk in the ceiling. It's probably nothing. Not a whorl of empty esophagus, thick, sleek, and reticulated.

Reindeer Cyclones

Stampedes are a dime a dozen. Any old day
something toothed can cast just one wisp of shadow,
and in a snap, the earth's throat is full of thunder.
Bye-bye, undusty air! See you later, Reason!
Did you know a herd of rhinos is called a crash?
That smash isn't special. It's what horned things do.
Even walruses poured onto the beach like
pink jugs of blubber will startle for crow-call,
peel out. One in ten won't pull through that
flippered thrash, that boil of whisker and tusk.

No ivory-bearer is immune, and I think I too
have pandemonium pulsing in my capillaries. I too
have tasted that longing to make a mad dash.
If I see one more fogging canister whetting the air
of a street lined with poster boards and little people,
I might not sit tight. Somewhere some woman
is saying *you don't believe me?* and lurching, all the
lights switching off in her brain. In Yemen,
babies are as gaunt as winter trees. We're not
meant to seal our ears to all this bleating.

Reindeer calves are born dark, their first fur
optimal for hiding out. Like all small young things,
they're at risk—but reindeer do danger differently.
Their reply to cracked twig or plucked bowstring
is not streak, not charge, but cyclone—a great
sweet twirl, a vast eddy in honor of those without
antlers. Their spiral of head and hoof says
there's something numbers can be good for.
When you watch that twist tightening on the tundra,
you'll know what kind of storm I want us to be.

Puffins

for Denise and for women everywhere

This auk is called the Clown of the Ocean,
but she's no joke. She can carry ten minnows
in her mouth, a whole flop of silver.
Nine islands have been named after her.
She rides the bracing northern tides
eight months out of the year,
can drink seawater that would conquer
the two shiny beans of your kidneys.
You can't sea-parrot her into performing
one dance she doesn't want to do.

Still, despite her splendor, she's known
to have apprehensive triangles for eyes,
and why, I am asking with an edge
to my voice, shouldn't she? In Iceland
they go on making enormous nets
to scoop her out of her own sky.
I hear the fresh heart of a puffin,
eaten raw, is Tradition. In the Faroes
her plucked pink bodies fill a fat table,
each snapped neck bright red. But

this bird doesn't wear her face for you.
Her spiny bill has beaconed in countless
oceanic dusks, fluorescent for reasons no one
understands. Who can say what whales
her pillowy breast has boated over, what
shipwrecks? She and meat don't share
the same dimension. You can't harvest this

spectacle of chroma and verve. She sees
colors you don't even know about, carries
a whole planet behind each eye.

Beach Days in Off Season

If there's anything I'm always in the mood for, it's Ocean,
and by Ocean I mean any salt coast, any boiling wake; Ocean
as in the crest of unsafe waters, the gray riot full of fish.

Every Ocean day we've had is one for the books, and by books
I mean I want to snap those days out of the Time Line, own
them the way we own the soap-dish shell we salvaged

from the January waves; the way sea owns sargassum;
the way we own each other with the tenderest care
in between our sheets. This is true even though I spend

at least half my time trying to decide what do with rage,
and beach days in off season are no exception. On our last
trip, I huddled into myself during the long drive back

like a homeless hermit crab. I did not want to say how the
molten pulse of anger had risen in me outside the retro arcade
with the Playboy machine, made every gull a Monster:

one who hungrily wants what cannot be owned—the body
and all its heat. I think there is nothing I want to own
except our days together: each stretch of shoreline

we've wandered in unsullied happiness, each cloud-wrapped
cliff top. If I lost this Land Ho! we've discovered hand in hand
I would be only an empty mussel shell, purple and flapping.

The Multi-Faceted Gem of Forgiveness Catches the Light

It's not about laying your fork and knife
next to the plate, parallel and always pointing
north, each steely tine seeming to say
I shall in all my best obey you, Madam.
It's not about the clouds that still hang on you.

It's not about stepping into sanctuaries with
thin lips and a belly full of lowliness. It's
not about saying yes. It's not about
unremembering the blue blooms you've seen
puddling under the pink skin that loves you.

It is about craving new eyes for every
living thing. May the toad see the cricket, may
the owl see the vole. May Claudius clap eyes
on his nephew at long last. May Hamlet see
Ophelia. May all the I'm sorries come out.

Lovesong with the Patriarchy Receding in the Distance

Every night before bed you suds the whole day's dishes in the sink,
and there are times when this frightens me still.
A man needs a kingdom to come home to—
I've been told by many tongues of different sizes and shapes
—or, as you'll quickly find out the hard way, he's bound
to stop coming home at all.

Most days we come home together
toting lunchboxes that carried the meals I made for us
in the plastic you'll soap and scrub.
The house is happy to see us, drowsing in its gentle disarray.
A squash bug buzzes behind the blinds.
The laundry I seldom have time to fold is burgeoning on the chair.

Sometimes you get angry, but you do not ask me
to put your anger in a little box labeled *testosterone*, tuck it into
    the closet
and pretend it does not exist.

We have stopped trying to be a man and a woman, a
fish and a bird, fire and water, pink and blue.

When you stop believing certain stories
they stop becoming true.

So long to the ladycage
after Lucille Clifton

means no more mincing   Enough
    of keeping things small

Means coming home knocking
finding for the first time in years
yourself in

she the radiant the standing up straight
she never letting a shoe pinch a toe   Nuh-uh
she untroubled by the gettingolder and its guests

Means open your mouth to speak
to this queen and your words
roll off her lips She's bright as a fall leaf   She's
saying *honey honey where
have you been?*

VII. What God Wants

Fourteen Reasons Not to Jump

Because you are young with many soft rains in front of you.
Because you are old with many soft rains behind you.
Because of the sharp blood of the trees and the smell
   of the ground that rises on every side.

Because of the bread in your cupboard that you left uneaten.
Because children have killed for bread.
Because the world is a great killing-field.
Because the world is a vast ball-room.
Because of the lilies of the field.

Because the green earth will never let you go.
Because she has always been like a gray miser chasing
   pennies across the tiles.
Because the royal and cerulean sky does not want you.
Because you have no wings.

Because out of diamonds gripping the ground
   comes the spring, a chorus of crocuses.
Because someday you may find a puzzle with five thousand
   pieces and put it together cardboard slice
   by cardboard slice.

Man's Search for Meaning

Once a month I tell my husband *I can't*
make it here: the hardness of people, the blue flies.
I want to open my eyes on a sun that's
not dying, on a world that knows me.

In spite of this, I have never considered
making an early departure. And the cows,
too, go on flicking their tails with
astonishing spunk under the orange sky.

Every time my retired professor emails me,
he is heading out to the homeless shelter.
He says *Viktor Frankl is right.* He says
Again late, I have to hurry off to CityLight.

Roofless

Been thinking a lot about People:
how fragile we each are, but it's a secret.
    Shhh don't tell

anyone you meet that you're little
also, that even the moon is nothing
but (*keep your voice down*) a battered stone.

Each day I pull a shirt over my chest
aware that this could be the sunup with my undoing
sitting in its mouth, but I don't say this I say
Gooooood Morning!

Most of the time we can't talk about
what's making us who we are:

> slammed doors, the walls that thicken
> between rooms in a ticking house

> in everyone the little mouth whimpering
> *love me*, the big mouth saying *watch this*

> the lies we've been told about all the
> big things: mostly our nation and sex

> God not picking up though we ring and
> ring—no one's certain he ever has

If I'm asking for anything
I'm asking for a light breeze, a finger flick.
I'm asking for just one playing card to go flying.

Oh, other Person, let's be roofless together
under our one moon's borrowed light
as long as it lasts.

Jackals

in the car with the heater running
cold on our hands
I told you I was losing my faith
*my faith my heart's child the light of my eyes
how I have nursed you
through the long fever nights
caressed your damp curls
don't go now*

in my boots the winter
crept like a desert jackal the engine
taking so long

when you think about Abraham that starfather
to three ways of grasping after God
is he standing under the silver frost
tail of the Milky Way
believing

or is he begging Sarah to go to bed
with another foreign king
please don't cry he says *I only
want to live*

in the night Abraham
keeps waking to the wails
of the fierce toothed jackals railing
at the white moon

where are you going? Sarah
is sitting up in the dark he knows
her eyes are ringed with wrinkles
she never trusts him anymore

and you said
do you think about Abraham
walking thirteen years
under the black sky
God not saying a word

Sleet

You know, I said, I've often thought life
is a long walk up a sleety street, and it's night.
You know what I mean? And it's just you and
my goodness, it's colder than anyone let on.
People pass you, but they're not people. At
the ends of leashes, dogs that are not dogs.

And here and there next to the plots of bones
we keep planting with almost no signs of spring,
steeples point their icy fingers.

O it's possible to be so lonely so lonely
the soul of your soul can quiver with
how lonely it is possible to be

and the lord Jesus at my elbow said
isn't that the truth?

Sure There's a God

" ... for else there's no delight."
　　—Thomas Traherne, "Insatiableness"

some people are saying they know that they know
and if you can't say the same well then come right
on up now don't be shy riiiiight up here be brave

there are things for which know is not the right
word but sometimes I can hardly bear living know
-ing dying could be waiting around any corner

o you blue years full of sky full of birds and the
ocean under the boat and the silk tablecloths in the
room of dancing—if you go away from me I shall

have nothing left and why have I walked this earth
if only to go away from you? when I grow sad after
lovemaking it's this I'm thinking of in each bone

but not the preacher he is not afraid of anything
he smacks the podium he says now with every head
bowed and every eye closed let's see those hands

What God Wants

I don't care what anyone says
not blood

not the steam rising from the hot pink muscles
splayed on the tarp
not the white fat that smells warm in the pan

they say wrath they say satisfy but
all my anger scatters when someone says *sorry*
I will do better and does it

when i learned about the camps the
nighttime raids the cattle prods
so many of my sisters who cannot speak who
can only lie down quietly
I cried for days
why do men always want to hurt us? I asked my pillow
surely we have not deserved this
but she didn't answer

still at this very moment I have it in me to sob
for a small frightened boy who became six feet tall
and informed me that women
are ruining everything

God's mercy I've been told is bigger than mine
but I've seen many bovines carved
and every time thought
no succulent rib no roast
sounds good to me now

Me and God are good buddies actually,

    (although I realize this may come as a surprise to you given
    what I am all the time saying on the subject of holy men)

both big fans of all the same things: evening walks in
summer weather, Planet Earth, the winter beach,

poems by earnest unbelievers, rabbits on the heathered
hills, dark scarves on the piping plovers skittering in the sea,

    (it's true: I don't like the word "holy," so often meaning
    abhorrence of the body God made me and likes a lot)

our many sisters from history who were never allowed
to speak—we understand them. We sit down quietly

for a long time next to their unraveled minds. Then I say
Say everything you want to say. Me and God have plenty of time.

    (so often meaning someone can enter this temple
    and somebody else cannot)

Me and God don't have time for your nonsense. We've got
places to be and things to do. *This sunrise is not gonna watch*

itself says God. Me and God are putting on our shoes.
It's looking like Another Great Day.

Look

when I start talking to God again
I'll say
look at the black trees sprouting
white lace look at the stars
in their fields
and he'll look

nobody ever
looks
that's nice they say
without looking

I was gone so long
God am I glad you're still here
God have I missed you

VIII. And Winks

manifesto on the
lifting of a lockdown

out of the saddest summer here we come
oh lord we are saying we are ready at last

comfort nor terror can stop us now
nor the field of blue crows at the top of the hill
tearing the flesh of the dead in the ordinary way

what you have learned no one can take from you
no one can wipe that better world from your eyes
wherever you look you see it looking back at you
it taps a finger to its nose and winks

Acknowledgments

I am heartily grateful to the editors of the following publications and productions in which many of these poems first appeared, some in earlier versions.

8 Poems: "Flipper"
Barrelhouse: "Pet Hates"
Beloit Poetry Journal: "Astronauts in Denmark"
Black Fox Literary Magazine: "Nightingale"
Blue Earth Review: "Free Pears"
Bracken: "The Mandalina Tree"
Chestnut Review: "Aşure (Noah's Pudding)"
Christian Century: "Sleet," "On the Cusp of the Pandemic," "On Not Losing You After All"
Cultivating: "Angry Dads," "Flourish: A Spencerian Definition," "manifesto on the lifting of a lockdown"
The Daily Poem Podcast: "Kabul Airport"
Delmarva Review: "Jackals"
DIALOGIST: "Collage of Airports"
Dillydoun Review: "Vibrant Photos That Show What the Middle East Is Really Like"
Dust Poetry Magazine: "Look"

Ekphrastic Review: "Hotel Window"

Ellipsis...Literature and Art: "At Last I Have It Out with France," "The Lizard King"

Fathom: "The Multi-Faceted Gem of Forgiveness Catches the Light"

Funicular: "Lovesong with the Patriarchy Receding in the Distance," "King's Cross Station"

Iron Horse Literary Review: "Summer of the Oystercatchers"

Juke Joint: "Wherever You Go Someone Has Been There Already"

The Mark Literary Review: "The Club of Imaginary Friends," "Alterations"

Pensive Journal: "10 Things I Learned in the '10s"

Pile Press: "So long to the ladycage"

Poetry Northwest: "On the 20th Anniversary of 9/11 a Lot of People Are Saying Never Forget"

Red Lemon Review: "Write a Poem About Coffee"

Red Rock Review: "Belen Köy"

Reunion: The Dallas Review: "Man's Search for Meaning"

Ruminate: "Fourteen Reasons Not to Jump"

SAND Journal: "Sure There's a God"

Sheila-Na-Gig Online: "Kukla Kebap," "Campus East"

Silk + Smoke: "Annie"

Stirring Lit: "Pulling Teeth," "Reindeer Cyclones," "Roofless"

The Sunlight Press: "An Ode to Everything"

Sweet Tree Review: "Wilfredo Speaks," "Three Things You Need to Get Through a Plague"

The Windhover: "The Table"

Welter: "Beach Days in Off-Season"

Notes

"Three Things You Need To Get Through a Plague" is after Tim Stanley's March 23, 2020, article "We were wrong: this isn't a war, it's a plague" in *The Telegraph*. My poem was written as a meditation on the following phrases from Stanley's piece: " ... a strong sense of oneself, a confidence in being alone, a hinterland ... "

 The italicized stanza in "At Last I Have It Out with France" is a direct quote from a Wikipedia article in which part of the quote is attributed to Sebö Endrödi's 1985 volume *The Dynastinae of the World*.

 "Vibrant Photos That Show What the Middle East Is Really Like" features Turkish and Arabic vocabulary that may be unfamiliar to some readers. Here is a glossary of these terms:
 gahwa: Arabic coffee
 rehal: a foldable bookrest for the Quran
 çay (pronounced like "chai"): traditional Turkish tea
 lokma: Middle Eastern pastries made of deep-fried dough
  soaked in syrup
 amca: Turkish for "uncle," also used as a term of respect for
  men of a certain age

The phrase "war is over if you want it" from "The Mandalina Tree" is a nod to John Lennon and Yoko Ono's 1969 poster campaign.

The *Tiny Poems for Afghanistan* were written in solidarity with the Afghan people mostly in August and September of 2021 as the United States government took heat for a botched withdrawal from Afghanistan after two decades of occupation fraught with chaos and civilian deaths.

In "Nightingale," the phrase "way down in Egypt land" comes from the traditional African-American spiritual "Go Down, Moses."

"The Multi-Faceted Gem of Forgiveness Catches The Light" contains multiple references to William Shakespeare's *Hamlet*. The line "I shall in all my best obey you, madam," is taken directly from Act 1, Scene 2.

Title Index

Numbers
10 Things I Learned in the '10s 25

A
Alterations 46
Angry Dads 79
Annie 40
An Ode to Everything 42
Arrival 66
Astronauts in Denmark 86
Aşure *(Noah's Pudding)* 49
At Last I Have It Out with France 36

B
Beach Days in Off Season 94
Belen Köy 50

C
Campus East 20
Collage of Airports 69

E

End Time 22

F

Flipper 81
Flourish: A Spencerian Definition 76
Fourteen Reasons Not to Jump 100
Free Pears 18

H

Hotel Window 67

J

Jackals 103

K

Kabul Airport 56
King's Cross Station 24
Kukla Kebap 30

L

Look 109
Lovesong with the Patriarchy Receding in the Distance 96

M

manifesto on the lifting of a lockdown 112
Man's Search for Meaning 101
Me and God are good buddies actually 108
Metamorphosis 70

N

Nightingale 88

O

One Kabul University Student Said 61

ong Live the Protestors in Dasht-e Barchī 59
On Not Losing You After All 68
On the 20th Anniversary of 9/11 a
    Lot of People Are Saying Never Forget 63
On the Cusp of the Pandemic 14

P

Pet Hates 89
Puffins 92
Pulling Teeth 87

R

Reindeer Cyclones 91
Roofless 102

S

Sleet 105
Social Exchange Theory 71
So long to the ladycage 97
Summer of the Oystercatchers 21
Sure There's a God 106

T

The Club of Imaginary Friends 32
The Lizard King 74
The Mandalina Tree 53
The Multi-Faceted Gem of
    Forgiveness Catches the Light 95
The Table 16
Third Culture 72
Three Things You Need
    to Get Through a Plague 15
to the people saying *but i was only a child*
    when we invaded Afghanistan 57
Two Blessings for the Citizens of an Empire 60

U

Unnecessary Promise 84

V

Vibrant Photos That Show What
the Middle East Is Really Like 44

W

What God Wants 107
When Anyone Speaks Up for the Bombs
I Want to Shout 64
when I see another woman in
Afghanistan has killed herself 62
Wherever You Go Someone Has Been There Already 38
Wilfredo Speaks 82
Write a Poem About Coffee 34

Y

your passport country 58

First Line Index

A

After years had sprouted, withered 50
all night we were crossing the ocean 24
All these years the clouds have been falling 38
although I realize this may come
   as a surprise to you given 108
an airport is a city where no one is staying 69
At any given time it's a tall order to find God 88

B

Because you are young with many
   soft rains in front of you 100
Been thinking a lot about People 102
But I was afraid 67

C

Coffee first came onto my scene when I was six 34

D

don't look away 56

E

Every day that summer 21
Every night before bed you suds the
 whole day's dishes in the sink 96

G

God is speaking to us but 25

H

Here, as everywhere, they seem to pursue us 79

I

I do not want to have anything against you, France 36
I don't care what anyone says 107
i for one am fonder than language 59
If there's anything I'm always in the mood for, it's Ocean 94
If you could go back, you would write 42
If you do not come up, I will go down after you 81
In Adana, the mandalinas are beginning to glow 53
i never forget the neighbor boy 63
In every way he can, he is saying his country is beautiful too 44
In my dream last night someone 22
In that springtime of long walks, I was always saying *Look* 20
in the car with the heater running 103
in the end I wonder 72
in the grocery store tonight 14
I see faster I see the rope the rat poison 62
is nothing to be proud of 58
It had to be a bad day for whomever had the job 86
It's not about laying your fork and knife 95
It was for a *Daboll's Arithmetick* that he walked so they say 76

J

Just a pet hate, of which I have many. They do no harm and give 89

L

listen can't you hear 57

M

means no more mincing Enough 97

O

On a fence 18
Once a month I tell my husband I *can't* 101
out of the saddest summer here we come 112

S

some people are saying they know that they know 106
Stampedes are a dime a dozen. Any old day 91

T

The day suddenly comes 46
the day you came 66
There are dreams where you feel your lungs filling 68
There is a loneliness in loose ends. All my friends 16
there is a wounded thing inside me going on about 30
They brought her home in hazelnut season 40
They destroyed the only bridge 61
This auk is called the Clown of the Ocean 92

V

Victorian women were warned to expect a tooth loss 87

W

what if one morning I woke up and I was 70
When he walked off the ark after 49
When I remember what has passed 71
when I start talking to God again 109
when we are parted I will leave 84
When we were children we knew very few people 32

when you pause for applause 60
Would you still love me 74

Y

Yes I know I have a name that 82
You know, I said, I've often thought life 105
You need three things to get through a plague, and 15
your we is somebody else's they 64

www.ingramcontent.com/pod-product-compliance
Lightning Source LLC
Chambersburg PA
CBHW011947150426
43193CB00019B/2926